P9-DDJ-066

ANDALUSIA

© OTERMIN. *Ediciones*

Telf. & Fax: (95) 229 56 42
D.L. MA. 707. 93.
ISBN. 84-88187-14-9

Distribución:
MINIDRUGSTORE, S.L.

Telf: (95) 222 77 07
Fax: (95) 222 01 44

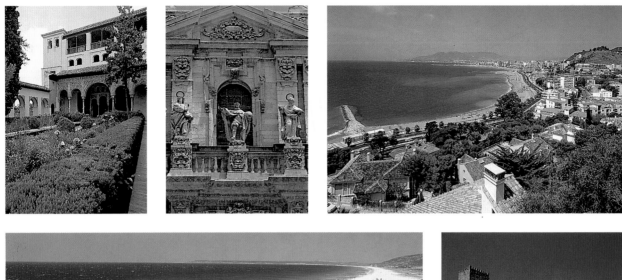

Andalusia is situated to the south of the Iberian Peninsula. Its area, the largest of all Spanish regions, is of 87.268 sq. kilometres, with a population of approximately 6.500.000 inhabitants. The following eight provinces belong to this Community: **Almería, Cádiz, Córdoba, Granada, Huelva, Jaén, Málaga** and **Seville.**

Its geography is typically mediterranean, with three very different orographic regions, which from north to south are as follows: Sierra Morena, a range of mountains which cross Andalusia from the east to the west and acts as a natural border with the castillian plateau: The Guadalquivir valley almost of triangular shape, which lies between Sierra Morena and the Betica mountains, and through which runs the river Guadalquivir collecting water falling from the Sierra Morena and from a major part of the Bética mountains: lastly the Bética mountain range which occupies almost half of the andalusian territory and runs along the mediterranean coast from Cape Gata in Almeria, to Gibraltar, Ronda, Las Alpujarras and Sierra Nevada all belong to this range of mountains. In Sierra Nevada one can find the highest point in the Iberian Peninsula, the Mulhacen (3.481 mt.)

Andalusia has the warmest climate in Spain. Mediterranean, mild and extremely dry in summer. Winters are mild and the average yearly temperature is 16° Celsius inland, an 18° C on the mediterranean coast.

Evidence of man in Andalusia goes back at least one million years to the Quaternarium period. In those days man hardly knew how to strike a stone to turn it into a sharp point or edge, which would serve to attack or to deffend himself from preying animals. The oldest human remains found in Andalusia date from 80.000 years the Neanderthalis Homo (first stage of Homo sapiens). Those early settlers looked for safety and shelter in caves and gradually learned the use of fire. There is extensive evidence of homo sapiens' presence in Andalusia. These men apparently came from Africa through the Gibraltar Straight, which in the Quaternarium could have been crossed on foot.

At the end of the last glacier period, the ice disappeared and so did the animals which were the main food source of those early hunters. Thus ends the paleolithic giving way to the neolithic age. Man undergoes a profound change, no longer using nature in a depradatory way but becoming its collaborator. At the end of the fifth millenium B.C. man changes his gathering nomadic society into a producer one. Agriculture probably came from Africa through Andalusia, to Europe.

With the emergence of the metal cultures, a big improvemen was seen in tools, arms, and other implements. The Andalusian mountain area, very rich in gold, silver, copper and other metals, soon occupies a privilidged trading position.

Eastern sailors developed ambitious travelling and colonising plans to ensure their commercial routes highly sought after metal markets. Their contemporary competitors the phoenicians and the greeks would also come to this area and would belome a decisive factor in southern Andalusian history.

Simultaneously, the kingdom of Tartessos starts to show signs of solid political unity, dominating the metal resources and becoming richer with the profit from demand and exploitation of extensive cattle and farm land.

The period between VI and III BC is a complex one and information on it is scarce, except concerning the carthagenians' important role in insuring their trade routes with the support of a powerful army.

From the middle of III BC Rome and Carthage had gone from their treaty discussions to open war. Occident domination was in dispute. After their first major defeat the carthagenians decided to occupy those territories farthest away from Rome. In the year 237 BC, **Amilcar,** a carthagenian general, landed in **Cádiz** and in the next ten years took control of all the Iberian south and southeastern territories. By then Tartessos had already been divided in several kingdoms, each with different degrees of power. On the other hand they kept to their original activities in the fields of economy, art and culture. In order to restrain the carthagenians, the Romans signed the Ebro Treaty. However **Hanibal, Amilcar's** son attacked **Sagunto** initiating the second war between Roma and Carthage.

Later **Hanibal** would cross the Alps trying to attack Rome from the most unexpected side, as far as the romans were concerned.

The struggle between Rome and Carthage for political control was at its most virulent in the Iberian Peninsula. In 206 BC, the roman general **Scipio,** nick-named *the African,* conquered the region which he named Bética after the river *Baetis* (Guadalquivir). Thus began the romanising process and the use of latin, which in those days was the language of cultural exchange. Philosophers such as **Séneca** and the first emperors who were born outside the roman peninsula, such as **Trajano** and **Hadrian,** all came from this roman province.

With the roman occupation the Iberian people became an integral part of historical mediterranean culture. The romans built roads to allow for the flow of their legions and traders, giving way to camps and cities which became important trade centres.

Around 411, the barbarians from the other side of the Rhine arrived in Andalusia, crossed the Gibraltar straight and occupied the African coast. Later in 458 they would be displaced by the visigoths. These new settlers inter mixed with the spanish-roman aristocracy, formed the first monarchy.

Around 711, an arab-berber army of some 12.000 men under **Tarik,** defeated the king of the visigoths, **Rodrigo,** on the shores of the river Guadalete (Cádiz) beginning the history of Al-Andalus. **Tarik,** after a harduous siege occupied **Córdoba** and continuing the roman road went on to **Toledo.** One year later a new army occupied **Carmona, Sevilla** and **Mérida.** By 716 nearly all of the spanish-visigoth population were entitled to keep their properties in exchange for paying taxes. The victors, some 30.000 arabs and berbers, were given land, initiating islamic settlements in Al-Andalus.

Al-Andalus is the name given by the arabs to their new domains and it is the origin of the word Andalusia, which was to become the centre of muslim Spain. Little by little a new civilization appeared, where different cultures and religions mixed.

In the year 755 **Abd-al-Rahman** declared the first independent Emirate. Society then was very homogenius and one could find, along with the political and economica aristocray, small traders, craftsmen and farmers, all of then enjoying a prosperous period. In 922 Al-Andalus reached its maximum cultural and economic splendour. During the caliphate **Córdoba** became the most populated city in occident.

The "Muladies" (muslims of spanish origin) resented because of ethnic discrimination, religious pluralism and regional differences, began an independence movement in the tenth century. This took place during the Omeya monarchy of Córdoba resulting in the disgregation into different taifa kingdoms. In spite of being militarily weak these kingdoms, very strong culturally, gave rise to the most splendied period ever achieved in muslim Spain.

During the eleventh and twelfth centuries new muslim invasions occured: the "Almoravide" and "Almohadi" invaders, taking advantage of the "Taifa" kingdoms' weakness, easily conquered them. Only the Seville and Granada kingdoms, berber dominated, could keep an historical continuity.

After **Las Navas de Tolosa** battle in 1212 and the conquests of **Fernando III** of Castille, all of Al-Andalus became part of the kingdom of Castille, except Granada, which would be conquered in 1492 by the **Catholic Monarchs** Fernando and Isabel. Granada held a privilidged position because it was on the route through which sudanese gold reached Castille. This gold was traded by the "Nazaríes" in exchange for oil, cloth. And weapons. The kingdom of the nazaríe only lasted as a result of castillian tolerance, whose interest was in maintaining taxes paid by Granada.

During the seven centuries of arab civilisation their influence in linguistics, farming, science and art was enormous. The arabs introduced a whole range of technical botanical and economic inovations. Some examples: watermills windmills, paper, silkworm cultivation, as well as a whole wide range of new perfumes and flavours unknown to the european continent: jasmin, saffron, rice, sugar, apricots, lemons, watermelons, aubergines, etc.

From XIII century and as a result of the conquests of **Fernando III** and **Alfonso X** the prosperous intensive farming of the river Guadalquivir started to be exploited extensively with olives and cattle as the basis. With the growth of turkish power, fear arose in relation to Granada and the possibility of it being the entry for a new muslim invasion of Europe. In a period of only eleven years the **Catholic Monarchs** were able to conquer all the territories of the kingdom of Granada, concluding with the fall of **Boabdil,** king of Granada.

During the XIII century the christian dominated majority co-existed with the jewish and ''Mudéjar'' ethnic minorities. Both of these minorities were subject to discriminatory laws and special taxes.

During XIV century north African and Canarian trade routes were opened up creating commerce in Andalusia, due to three main reasons: firstly **Sevilla's** geographic situation allowed boats of upto 300 tons to reach the sea through the Guadalquivir. In the XV century tonnage increased and ports such as **Sanlúcar de Barrameda, Puerto de Santa María** and **Cádiz** became increasingly important. Second was the Andalusian agricultural richness in oil, cereals, leather, chickpeas, wool, honey, skins, cheese and wine. The third and decisive factor was the existence of a rich nobility and merchants who were in control of foreing trade.

There were various atlantic routes with **Seville:** the coast route with Portugal (wine, wheat, and figs in exchange for cork and fruits) emphasized by Portugal's African territories; the Cantabrian route which during the XV century allowed for commerce with Galician, Cantabrian and basque people (fish, iron and wood were exchanged for oil, cereal and wine).

Atlantic Andalusia soon became the most important area in the kingdom of Castille, in economic terms. Because of this, agricultural production was stimulated, capital was invested, work encouraged and knowledge of maritime routes was enormously improved.

The different cultures that have left their marks on this land have contributed to create this individual open and hospitable people who have assimilated through centuries a special knowledge and culture.

ALMERIA

This eastern Andalusian province is made mainly of two mountain ranges. The Sub-béticas range in the north and Penibética in the south, separated from each other by the Almanzora valley. The coast mountains of Gata, Cabrera and Almagrera towards the east, finishing in high cut out cliffs, whereas in the south, from Gata Cape onwards, the coast line is flat and sandy opening up in to the **Almeria** bay.

This province climate is very dry. Rains are very scarce and its average yearly temperature is 18° C. Winters are mild with 12° C as an average, whereas summers are very hot with an average of 24° C. Only in the highest parts of the mountains temperatures of 13° C are reached; vegetation is sub-tropical, "Pita", cactus, and young

Almería. View from the port

La Alcazaba

La Alcazaba

The Cathedral

Cathedral's interior

palm shoots , being species which can withstand drought, and only in the highest mountains can we find pinetrees and evergreen oaks.

The mineral richness of this region was to originate pre-historic settlements such as ''Los Millares'' and ''El Argar''. **Almería** City is of phoenecian origin, who named the port city *''Urci''.* This port was the basis for their metal trade. With the romans arrival it became one of the most important and was called *''Portus Magnus''.*

Almeria's maximum splendour came with the arabs, especially during the Cordobese Omeya Emirate. They called the city *Al-Miriya* (the mirror), thus giving **Almería** its present name. During **Abderraman III** this city grew very much and after the fall of the Córdoba Emirate, when **Almanzor** died, it became an independent emirate which spread itself in the XI century throuh parts of **Granada, Córdoba, Jaén** and **Murcia.**

It was then, one of the richest cities in Europe, after **Córdoba** and **Constantinopla.** In 1147 **Alfonso VII** of Castille conquered the city and the kingdom. However 10 years later it was again conquered by the arabs. In 1498 Fernando and Isabel the Spanish **Monarchs** finally dominated it. From the moment of this conquest on, a period of economic decline started in **Almería,** aggravated by the expulsion of the ''moriscos''. The fields were abandoned by the population, despite the fact that christians re-settlers came from everywhere in Spain. Until 1822 it was part of the so called Kingdom of Granada until Parliament determined the boundaries of this reign, which have been maintained to the present day.

Almería started to recover its economic importance in the XIX century when the Gador mines were discovered, resulting in the arrival of the railway and the construction of the port.

Mojácar and **Roquetas de Mar** are two interesting historic-touristic cities of this province.

La Alcazaba, the most important monument in **Almería,** dates from the muslim occupation period. It was built by **Abderraman III** in the VII century and was extended by **Almanzor** in the X century. It stands on the top of a hill from which the bay and the whole city can be seen. The Cathedral is a typical example of a late gothic temple-fortress (1524-1543). In the facade four large pillars stand out. Also important are the two main doors, the coral dome the sacristy, the cross, and grand altar with different chapels. Santiago el Viejo, San Pedro and San Juan Churches are also important monuments.

Gata-Nijar Natural Park stands to the east a few kms. from the capital. It was created in 1987 and has an area of 29.000 hectares occupying parts of the **Almería, Carboneras** and **Nijar** districts. It is the place to enjoy a varied shore line full of small bays, cliffs, reefs and immense white sandy beaches.

Panoramic view from Sierra Cabrera

Agua Amarga

Mojácar beach

Vélez Blanco

Vélez Blanco castle

Tabernas

View from theTabernas castle

Cabo De Gata

Los Genoveses beach

Agua Amarga beach

Agua Amarga

'élez Blanco

Lucainena de Las Torres

Natural Park Cabo De Gata-Níjar

Vélez Blanco

Mojáca

Port of Garrucha

Gata lighthouse ▼

Mojácar   Carboneras

Acosta Saltmines ▼

CADIZ

Cádiz province is situated to the southern vortex of the Iberian Peninsula, its eastern shoreline bathed by the Mediterranean and the western by the Atlantic.

The geography of Cádiz includes three large regions. To the east a mountainous area, where Grazalema and Ubrique stand out, both converging in the Tarifa Point: to the north, the marshes and finally in the shores, two important bays, **Cádiz,** a low and sandy bay with many dunes caused by atlantic winds and Algeciras bay in the Gibraltar Straight.

Three rivers flow through this province into the Atlantic: Guadalquivir, Guadalete

Cádiz. La Caleta beach

Genovés Park

Monument to Moret

Puerta de Tierra. Details

La Victoria beach ▼

and Barbate, and the Guadiaro river flowing between **Cádiz** and **Málaga** into the Mediterranean. Because of its southern position in the Iberian Peninsula, Cádiz has played an important role in history, serving as a bridge between the european and African continents and as a gateway to the Atlantic Ocean.

Cádiz is one of the oldest western european cities, its origin going back more than 300 years. It was a prosperous carthagenian colony and one of the most important trade ports since it was a compulsory stop-over for all ships on their route towards the Atlantic, as a result favouring trade with the Guadalquivir valley. **Cádiz** prosperous position (**Cádiz** *Gadez, Gadir*) was maintained during the roman period. But was interrupted at the time of muslim invasion, when a frontier which ran through the plains villages was formed facing the mountain area of the Kingdom of Granada. Some of these villages still keep their nickmame: ''La frontera'' (the frontier) such as in **Arcos, Chiclana, Jerez** or **Vejer de la Frontera. Cádiz** was finally re-conquered in 1265. However it didn't recover its trade posperity until the XVI century when it became the port wich would channel important trade with America. In 1558 ships coming from the Antilles with leather and sugar cargoes were allowed to disembark in Cádiz. Permission was also extended to all ships which would arrive with technical problems from their atlantic voyage and could not cross the Guadalquivir sandy barrier, on their way to **Seville**. This problems would gradually condition the importance of the port of **Cádiz,** especially when the american goods started to be carried in larger vessels. Moreover this was the foreing traders favourite port on account of its more extensive facilities in comparison with **Seville**.

It is therefore easy to understand that when the plague epidemics took place by the middle of XVII century and devastated **Cádiz** and **Seville,** the latter started on its way to decadence whereas **Cádiz** was soon to re-cover from the crisis.

After the french invasion had taken place, in the beginning of XIX century, Parliament was transferred to **Cádiz** by government decree in 1811. It was a positive period for Parliament and sound laws were drawn up. They started by proclaiming national sovereingty by incorporating into the nation the jurisdictional counties, resulting in the abolition of feudalism. They also drafted laws on printing, abolishing

Cathedral   Cathedral. Interior   Beach at the Cape of Trafalgar ▶

censorship and surpresed the Inquisition, and the political Constitution of the Spanish Monarchy was drawn up.

The most important monument in **Cádiz** is the Cathedral, whose building was started in 1720. It has three naves, two lateral chapels, cross, dome and ''Girola''. Santa Cruz, Santo Domingo, Carmen and San Agustin are all important churches. The archeological Museum has a wide variety of pre-historic remains together with some from Carthage, Greece, and Rome along with paleo-christian and visigoth items.

In this province there are other very interesting cities, from a historic point of view: **Algeciras, Arcos de la Frontera, La Línea, Puerto de Santa María, San Fernando, Sanlúcar de Barrameda, Tarifa** and **Vejer.**

The **Natural Park of Barbate,** a maritime inland Park, is situated on the Atlantic Coast, at the entry of the Straight of Gibraltar. It serves as a rest area for migratory birds which occupy the river Barbate marshlands for this purpose.

Cádiz bay, which was declared a Natural Park in 1989 has an extension of approximately 10.000 hectares and is formed by beaches and marshland caused by fluvial sediments. Its important fauna includes mainly migratory birds. UNESCO has declared the **National Park Sierra de Grazalema** as a Biosphere Reservation. Its extension is of some 51.000 hectares and it is situated to the west of the Baetic Range of mountains, extending through the mountain area of Cádiz and through part of the Serrania de Ronda in the Málaga province.

The **National Park Los Alcornoques** (cork trees) has an area of 170.000 hectares which extends from Tarifa in the south to the northeast of Málaga province. It has the largest cork-trees wood in the whole of the Iberian Peninsula and is one of the most important in the world.

Cork trees

Arcos de la Frontera ▼

River Barbate

Grapevines in Jerez de la Frontera

Sierra de Grazalema

Arcos de la Frontera. Church of Santa María

El Bosque. Scenery

erez de la Frontera. Street market

Panoramic view from Vejer de la Frontera

Grazalema

Sanlúcar de Barrameda

Benamahoma

View of the african coastline from Tarifa

Bay of Bolonia ▼

rafalgar lighthouse

Barbate. Port

Los Caños de Meca ▼

Beach of Tarifa

CORDOBA

The province of **Córdoba,** through which flows the Guadalquivir in its middle course, is the most northern of all andalusian provinces. Its geography includes in the North, Sierra Morena, La Campiña in the centre, and the Cordilleras Subbéticas in the south. As the province is surrounded by mountains and has no maritime influence, its climate is mediterranean and continental. Average yearly temperatures reach around 19° C with

Córdoba   The Mosque - Cathedral. Interior view ▶

mild winters (average 10° C) whereas summers are extremely hot, often reaching 45° C and above.

Córdoba city is situated on the right bank of the river Guadalquivir and it was always an important communications crossroads: Extremadura heading west across the sierra, the route to the Meseta, crossing the Sierra Morena through **Despeñaperros,** and the Via Augusta which ran along the river Guadalquivir upto **Cádiz,** passing through **Seville.** This city's situation in the Bético Valley, in the confluence area between the Sierra and La Campiña, determined its importance as a trading and cultural centre for the region.

Córdoba, the capital of this province was founded by the carthagenians. It began its splendour period around 169 BC due to **Claudio Marcelo's** decision to establish there a roman colony. Córdoba's strategic situation and rich agriculture have undoubtely contributed to its development. By 584 it became a meeting point for the bysantines and visigoths. During muslim occupation in 716 **Córdoba** was the capital of Al-Andalus. By 756 it became the Emirate's capital and in 929 the Caliphate's. All these circumstances contributed to the city's growth, occupying a larger area than it does at present. It was the most populated western city with more than 250.000 inhabitants. By comparison, **Toledo** had around 37.000 inhabitants, **Almería** 27.000, **Granada** 26.000, **Zaragoza** 17.000, and **Valencia** and **Málaga** 15.000 inhabitants each. The urban organization was as seen in all muslim cities. The public granary, the ''alcaicería'' the markets and the baths were situated around the mosque (Mezquita Mayor).

Economic activity was based on farming and cattle. Cereal and pulse cultivation were outstanding and the surpluses of olives, raisins and figs were exported to the east. By the X century there were already windmills and the farming of rice, oranges and sugarcane had already been introduced.

▼ Details of the Mosque - Cathedral ▶

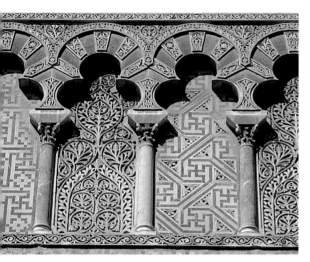

The crafts industry was centred in the manufacture of luxury items, such as gold, ivory and jade carvings. In the XI century two new industries appear: paper and glass. The knowledge of the latter was kept secret, which allowed Al-Andalus to maintain for several centuries a monopoly of a certain type of glass.

The most important monument of this period is the Mezquita Mayor. It was started around 780 by **Abd-al-Rahman** and was finished by **Almanzor** who extended it to the east with eight new naves. At present it occupies a rectangular area of 180 m. from north to south and 130 east — west. The majority of its columns were used from previous roman, paleo-christian and visigoth buildings. After the city's conquest in 1236 by **Fernando III,** christian consecration determined some changes in the mosque's interior in order to transform it in a cathedral. Some of these changes were the building of the royal chapel and other wall chapels, and the adaptation of the Chandelier.

Other important monuments in the city of **Córdoba** are: the Catholic Monarchs' Alcazar, which was built by **Alfonso XI** in 1328. The synagogue also built by **Alfonso XI** in 1315, is one of the three existing in Spain and the only one in Andalusia.

Lucena, Montilla and **Puente Genil** are also interesting cities from an historic point of view.

The **Natural Park of Cardeña** y **Montoro** belongs to Sierra Morena and is situated to the northeast of the cordobese province. One of the characteristics of this Park is "Las Bolas" (the balls), rounded granite blocks with diametres of approximately 1 mt.

The **Natural Park of Hornachuelos** is situated to the west of the province. Its name is derivated from the dark colour of its grounds, mainly slate. Its area is of 67.000 hectares and species like the black stork and the iberian linx are part of the local fauna.

Roman bridge over the river Guadalquivir   The Mosque - Cathedral. Interior ▶

Aguilar de la Frontera

Cabra. La Asunción church ▼

Montilla. Cruz Conde wine cellars

Montemayor. Landscape ▼

Lucena fields

Montoro

Montemayor ▼

Córdoba. Monument to Ben Hazam

Vineyards in Montemayor

Landscape in Lucena

Sunflowers in El Carpio

Lucena. San Mateo church

Córdoba. South façade of the Mosque - Cathedral ▼

Benamejí ▼

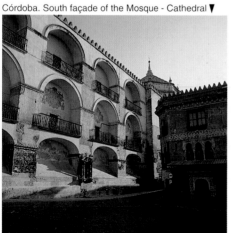

Lucena. El Carmen church ▼

◄ Córdoba. Monument to archangel San Rafael

Benamejí

Lucena. El Carmen church

Cabra ▼

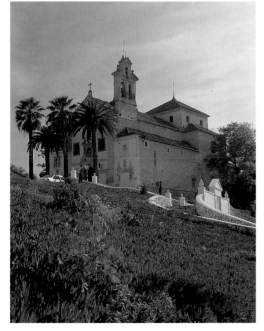

GRANADA

Granada province is situated between **Málaga** and **Almería** in the mediterranean side, touching the provinces of **Jaen, Albacete** and **Murcia** to the north, and **Córdoba** to the west. Near **Granada** city there was the Iberian city Elvira which became the capital of one of Al-Andalus provinces, remaining until the berber revolt in 1009-1010.

Grenade

La Alhambra ►

Its population was then forced to emigrate to nearby **Granada,** settling in the Alhambra and Albaicín hills and on the flats watered by the rivers Darro and Genil.

After the fall of the cordobese omeya caliphate there followed the **Granada** reign of "zíries" and at the end of the X century the "Almoravides" took control of this kingdom and were later dominated by the "Almohades". Once the "Almohade" decadence set in, a member of the **Baner-Al-Ahman** family conquered **Granada** in 1238, installing the "Nazaríes" dynasty which was in power for two and a half centuries and whose kingdom spread all the way into **Málaga** and **Almería** province.

Many muslims, among whom those escaping from the re-conquered Castillian territories, joined this new kingdom, re-populating and enriching what was to become the final muslim dominated area in the Iberian Peninsula. **Granada** became a large rich city with several mosques and palaces like the Alhambra. The kingdom of "Nazaries" wealth was ensured by the intensive silk industry, commerce with the east and Africa, and sudanese gold brought into Europe through **Granada.** After capitulation before the **Catholic Monarchs** in 1492 there would be no major changes in the area, since the surrender conditions allowed for the Granada people to keep their wealth, their laws, their habits and religion besides having command in part of the city. But stipulations were violated and in the six years after the city's conquest a division had already been made, establishing 2 different zones, one christian the other muslim. (Morería). The "Moriscos" group who controled the silk industry inspired the rebelion which

View of Granada from La Alhambra
Interior details of La Alhambra ▶

occurred in 1568 and which resulted in the expulsion of all ''Moriscos'' settled in the Albaicin.

During the muslim occupation Granada reached its most splendorous period under ''Nazarí'' occupation (1241-1492). The most representative monuments of that period are la Alhambra, the most important muslim palace actually remaining and the Generalife, the monarchs summer residence. In relation to fortress and military architecture Puerta Elvira stands out, this door closing the XIII century precint; la Alcazaba also from XIII century, and the Alcazar from the XIV century. The **Catholic Monarchs** had started and important artistic focus in the city, which was to be continued by **Carlos V** who ordered the building of a palace within the Alhambra. As far as christian art is concerned, the most important monument is the cathedral, the maximum example of Spanish Renaissance. Among the most representative civil buildings, the Royal Hospital founded by the Spanish Monarchs in 1504. The principal city Museums are: the Provincial Archaelogic Museum, the Alhambra's, the Provincial Fine Arts and the Town Hall's and the Cathedral's.

Besides the cathedral there are other important religious monuments, such as San José church gothic-mudejar, built on top of what was a mosque. La Cartuja, San Juan de Dios church, San Jerónimo monastery, etc.

Baza, Guadix, Motril and **Orjiva** are other province historical sites.

To the east of the province, ending at the **Almería** province, there is the **National Park of the Sierra de Baza,** forming part of the cordilleras Béticas. With altitudes from 1.200 to 2.200 meters its vegetation is adapted to strong winds and low temperatures.

The **Natural Park of Sierra Nevada** with an area of some 17.000 hectares occupies larger part of the Granada province (and also of that of **Almería**). It is rigt at the centre of the Penibética range of mountains. It is the largest mountain area in the Iberian Peninsula, which has a proper structural unity. It has more than twenty points higher than 3.000 mts., the highest in the Peninsula being the Mulhacen, with 3.481 mtrs. These heights are only surpassed in Europe by the Alps.

Generalife gardens

Cathedral. South façade

Cathedral. Interior

Catedral. Royal Chapel ▼

La Calahorra

El Negratín. Dam ▼

Baza

La Calahorra ▼

Guadix. Las Cuevas neighbourhood

Sierra Nevada ▼

Granada. La Alcaicería

Granada. La Alhambra gardens

Baza. Mayor church

Baza

Crops at the foot of Sierra Nevada ▼

Juviles

Pampaneira

Sierra Nevada

Calahonda ▼

HUELVA

The most western of all Andalusian provinces, bordered by the Portuguese frontier to the west, to the north with Extremadura, with **Seville** and **Cádiz** to the east and southeast, and with the Atlantic to the south.

Though **Huelva** is located in what is referred to as ''Dry Iberia'' its Atlantic frontal coastline allows for some relative humidity. Its main agricultural regions are on the plains, where cereals, vines and olives trees grow.

Huelva territories were settled by primitive mediterranean civilisations. It was an important commercial area for both the phoenecians and carthagenians on account of

Cathedral

48

La Concepción church

La Rábida Monastery. Interior

El Rocio ▼

its mineral wealth **(Calañas, Rio Tinto** and **Tarsis)** especially the mining of copper and iron pyrites.

During muslim occupation two taifa kingdoms were formed in the area, **Niebla** and **Huelva** being their main centres. By the middle of the XIII century the Castillians reconquered this area, establishing the southern frontiers of the Peninsula, this slowing lusitanian expansion. Huelva was originally a land of miners and farmers but their people would also become sailors, witnessing the initial discovery and subsequent conquest of América. Although the Colombian expeditions set off from this coast, the American commercial routes didn't pass through the area, following instead the Guadalquivir river towards Seville. So this western part of Andalusia would be forgotten until the XIX century when intense mining arrived.

Alfonso X reconquered Huelva in 1257 and passed it on to his daughter **Doña Beatriz de Guzmán,** the widowed portuguese queen. In the XV century it finally came under spanish control. Huelva territories were integrated from an administrative point of view into the kingdom of Seville. Until 1833, where the present borders were established including parts of the kingdom of Seville and a small part of Extremadura.

Palos de la Frontera is the port from where the three ships of **Columbus** expedition sailed off to the discovery of America. **Palos de la Frontera** is eleven kms. far from **Huelva** and the monastery of La Rábida is nearby.

Huelva city is situated between the mouths of the rivers Odiel and Tinto and the traces of its historic past were erased by several earthquakes during the XVIII century. Its monuments are relatively few. However San Pedro's church, La Merced convent with its XVIII century church, San Francisco's and Nuestra Señora de la Cinta sanctuary, deserve a mention.

Almonte, Aracena, Ayamonte, Cortejana, Cumbres Mayores and **Jabugo** are other cities of historic-touristic interest.

In 1964 the Coto Doñana biologic station was created and five years later it was declared **National Park "Entorno de Doñana".** At present it is the largest fauna centre of all Europe. Its special characteristics such as mild temperatures (13° C in winter and 30° C in summer) its physical structure of mobile dunes and marshes which in the past flooded the river Guadalquivir, made the region a place where more than 150 bird species spend the winter. The Park with the various smaller parks it includes, occupies an area of some 75.000 hectares to the south of the Huelva province.

The **Natural Park Sierra de Aracena** and **Picos de Aroche** are situated to the north of the province in the Sierra Morena most western area. This Park covers 184.000 hectares, mainly foothills where predominate slate and quartz giving the landscape its dark colour. The Iberian black stork and the Iberian linx are common to this area.

Isla Canela beach

Ayamonte. Fishing port

▲ Ayamonte. Details ▼▲

Bridge over the river Guadiana ▼   Alajar. Sierra de Aracena ►

Lepe. The river Piedras

Ayamonte. Sports port

Mouth of the river Guadiana ▼

Landscape in Sierra de Aracena

Jabugo. Hams drying up place

Aracena

Cortegana. Castle

Huelva. Bullring

National Park Doñana ▼

JAEN

This province is bordered to the north by the community of **Castilla-La-Mancha**, **Granada** to the south and **Córdoba** to the west. It is made up of three areas. Sierra Morena to the north, the Guadalquivir valley in the centre and the Subbéticas mountains to the south.

As a result of the Atlantic winds coming through the Bética valley, its climate is mild. Summers are very hot and winters are fresh on the plains and a bit colder in higher areas. The capital, situated at the junction of the Bética valley and the Subbéticas mountains is also the meeting point of two well defined regions: **"La Campiña"** and **"Los Montes"**, to the north and south respectively. The old city of *Aurgui* (the roman *Aurgui*) was a rich city on account of its fertile soil and silver mines. It was part of the Carthagenian empire and was converted into a fortress by them. During the second punic war, around

Jaén

Cathedral

National Parador ▼

Cathedral. Interior

Entry to National Parador ▼

270 B.C. it was conquered by **Lucio Scipio.** Under roman domination it was joined to the jurisdiction of the convent of **Ecija**, later becoming a township which was granted the tribute of flavia. This took place in the year 74 ad under the mandate of the roman **Vespasiano.**

In 712 it was conquered by the arabs, who changed its old name to *Geen*, the origin of its present day name. During muslim occupation this city's most brilliant period was under the caliphate. It was again converted to a fortress town and palaces and mosques where built. (Alcazar) after the fall of the caliphate its domains became property of the taifa kingdoms of Seville and later was occupied by the "Almoravides" and by the "Almohades". In 1246 it was ceded to **Fernando III** by agreement between the dominion of Granada and the kingdom of Castille. This would provoke the departure of muslim population towards arab domains. The control of this fortress had the important strategic value allowed for castillian domination of high Andalusia.

Jaén's province played a major historic role since through **Despeñaperros** contact between the castillian plateau and Andalusia was made possible. **Despeñaperros** played once more an important role in the **Bailén** battle since it prevented the access of Napoleon's army to **Andalusia.**

Jaén's oldest monuments belong to the muslim period. The arab baths date from the beginning of the 11th century. Santa Catalina's castle was re-built after the reconquest and presently maintains the majority of its walls as well as the allegiance tower and Santa Catalina's Chapel (XIII-XV).

On the site of the old mosque a Cathedral was built whose sacristy is one of the major achievements of spanish renaissance architecture. Other relevant religious monuments are the churches of San Andrés, San Ildefonso and Santa Magdalena.

The province museum contains important remains from the neolithic, Iberian, roman, spanish-arab and renaissance periods.

Andújar, Baeza, Linares and **Ubeda** are other important cities of historic interest.

The **Natural Park of Sierra Cazorla, Segura** and **Las Villas** is situated to the northeast of Jaén's province. It has an area of more than 200.000 hectares and is the largest protected area in Spain. Two rivers flow from these mountains: Guadalquivir and Segura running into the Atlantic and Mediterranean, respectively. 1.300 species of plants, 24 of them unique have been included in the floral catalogue of this area. Concerning wildlife there are various species of preying mammals, such as the fox, "Jineta", garduña birds of prey and one of the largest reservations in the Iberian peninsula of entomologic species.

The **Natural Park of Sierra Mágina** is situated in **La Campiña** area spreading its 20.000 hectares through the highest massif of the province (2.167 mt.) containing some flora species unique in the world.

◄ Sierra de Cazorla

Ubeda. El Salvador church

Andújar. San Miguel church

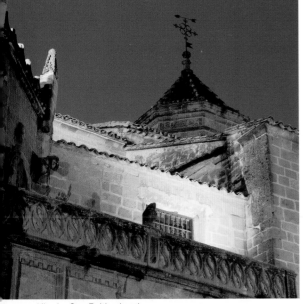

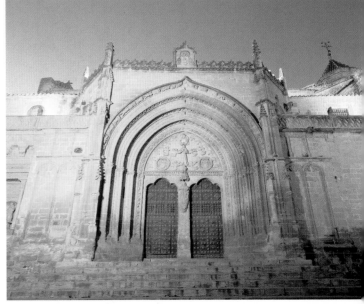

Ubeda. San Pablo church

Park in Ubeda ▼

Ubeda. San Pablo church

Baeza. Cathedral's interior ▼

Cazorla ►

Views of the Natural Park of Sierra de Cazorla and El Tranco dam ▲▼

Ubeda. Landscape

Olive grove in Cazorla ▼

Olive trees in Sierra de Cazorla

 ▲ Sierra de Cazorla ▼ ►

Cazorla

Baeza

Baeza. Jabalquinto Palace

Belenda ▼

Quesada ▼

Cazorla

Andújar

Cazorla. Castle

Cazorla

Don Pedro ▼

MALAGA

The boundaries of this province are **Sevilla** and **Córdoba** to the north, **Granada** to the east, the mediterranean sea to the south and **Cádiz** province to the west. Its climate is mediterranean with mild winters 12° C. and hot summers 25° C.

Many traces of pre-historic cultures going back to the bronze age can be found both in Málaga city and in the province. The group of burial stones in **Antequera** is the oldest in Europe. In the **Nerja** caves there are pre-historic black, yellow and red paintings.

The origins of **Málaga** city go back to the phoenecians and greeks who founded the *Mainake* colony near this city. In 205 B.C. it was a roman ally and become a roman city under the emperor **Vespasiano**. However this city's trading character would continue despite roman domination. Its foreign trade was based on the export of oil, cereal, wood, raisins, salt foods, wine and also slaves, developing a strong commercial capitalism controled by jews and syrians. Around the year 570 the city was taken from the bysantines by **Leovigildo**. The jewish and spanish-roman colonies carried on their commerce with Africa, Italy, Greece and Asia minor.

Málaga

La Alcazaba

Cathedral

Municipal Corporation

Cathedral. Interior

City's night view ▼

Las Tres Gracias fountain ▼

Abd-al-Aziz conquered the city in 714-716. Under the Caliphate Málaga was one of the 21 Khoras or territorial areas, of Al-Andalus. It achieved great prosperity in this period. Its population 15.000 at the end of the X Century with an urban bourgeoisie composed mainly of jews and muladíes. After the first taifas and the "Almoravides" and "Almohades" invasions it became a part of the kingdom of Granada and became in fact its main port. In 1487 it was conquered by the **Catholic Monarchs** who granted the city its charters (laws and population) and at the same time re-established its commercial relationship with the north of Africa.

During the XVI century **Málaga** and **Alicante** were the two main wool ports of Castille in the mediterranean. The moorish revolts in 1501 and 1586, their expulsion around 1611 together with the general decadence of spanish economy during the XVII century contributed to a decline in commerce, which was left in the hands of the english and dutch. It was not until XVIII Century that this region recovered its trading activities.

From the roman dominated period, the remains of the theatre are conserved and from the arabs "La Alcazaba" joined by a passage to the Gibralfaro fortress. The Cathedral was first built on the site of the Mezquita mayor but in 1528 a new building with three very high naves was started. Other interesting religious monuments are the Churches of Sagrario, Virgen de la Victoria and archbishops' palace. In the archaelogic museum of the Alcazaba one finds pre-historic remains of roman and mediterranean cultures.

Costa del Sol is the name given to the 300 Kms. of mediterranean coastline belonging to **Málaga** province. This southern strip which develops at the foot of Serranía de Ronda and Sierra Nevada, extends itself from **Estepona** to **Motril** (Granada). In the early sixties these sunny beaches saw the beginning of a tourist boom which resulted in the building of many hotels, restaurants, nautical ports, etc.

Antequera, Estepona, Fuengirola, Marbella, Mijas, Nerja, Ronda, Torremolinos and **Vélez-Málaga** are interesting from a touristic and historical point of view.

The **Natural Park Montes de Málaga** is situated to the north of the city of **Málaga**. This Park has an area of 5.000 hectares and has been re-forested with pinewoods planted in the basin of the river Guadalmedina in order to avoid the floods which, during centuries have devastated the capital.

The **Natural Park Sierra de las Nieves** is situated in the Serranía de Ronda. Its area is of more than 18.000 hectares. Its main morphological characteristics are deep gorges of more than 100 mts. and abysses which reach a depth of 1.100 mts. La Torrecilla, the highest point of this Park (1.919 mts.) is situated in the Sierra Blanca de Tolox. Some 3.000 hectares of this Park are covered with a particular type of silver fir, the "Pinsapo" this species can only be found in the subbéticas mountains and in the north of Africa.

Easter Week

Park in Málaga

Benalmádena. Chorpus Festivity

Ronda

Gaucín

Ronda canyon

Montejaque dam ▼

Ronda bullring ▼

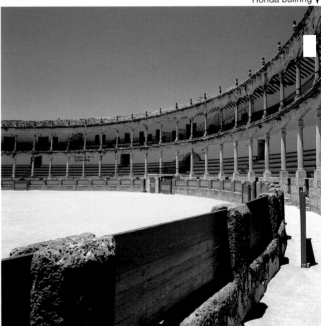

Gaucín

Casares

▲ Antequera ▼

Antequera. Menga cave

Antequera. El Torcal

rchidona

Frigiliana

asabermeja

Fuente de Piedra lagoons ▼

Nerja cave

Estate in Costa del Sol

Mijas

Marbella. Golf course ▶

Marbella

Torremolinos

Marbella. Port

Benalmádena. Port

Marbella. Beach ▼

Puerto Banús

Nerja

Sotogrande. Port

Estate in Costa del Sol

SEVILLE

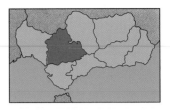

The boundaries of the province of **Seville** are as follows: **Badajoz** to the north, **Córdoba** to the northeast, **Málaga** to the southeast, **Cádiz** to the south and **Huelva** to the west. The province's geography is conditioned by the basin of the river Guadalquivir which crosses the whole province towards the southwest. Its climate is Mediterranean, with average temperatures of between 18° C and 16° C, with long hot summers.

The archaelogic remains found in **Seville** go back to the neolithic age. The city's history starts with its founders, the iberian tribes (Turdetanos) later, Seville was colonized by the phoenecians, greeks and carthagenean who fortified it with walls and towers as well as laid the foundations of its trade development. Around 205 B.C. the romans conquered it. In 48 B.C. **Scipio the African** founded Italica nearby. **Cesar** named it the capital of Bética raising *Hispalis* (Seville) to the status of a roman colony. **Augustus** granted it the privilidge to mint coins. After romanisation a series of germanic invaders settled in this region, first the vandals and later the sueves and in 513 it was incorporated to the visigoth kingdom. In 712 it was besieged and conquered by the muslims who named it *Isbiliya*, the origin of its present name. Under arab domination the city underwent a great number of urbanistic changes. Under the first "Almohade" domination the mezquita mayor and its minaret "La Giralda" were built (1172-1182).

Sevilla

La Giralda ▶

During the reign of the **Catholic Monarchs** there began in **Seville** a new splendorous period which would continue under **Carlos V** and **Felipe II**. The Cathedral was built. The first crown printers were established at the university and the city also became very important in the field of industry and the arts. This great success and the fact that **Seville** became the principal city of the kingdom, was undoubtely due to the port; point of arrival and departure of all of the expeditions to the new world, especially once the ''Casa de la Contratación de las Indias'' was created in 1503. **Seville** became in some ways the centre of the world, its population increasing from 60.000 to 115.000 (1588) by the middle of the XVII century starts the city's decline, accentuated by the pest epimedics, in 1649 which killed around 60.000 people, and the transfer to **Cádiz** of the ''Casa de Contratación''. **Seville** did not recover from this decadence until the beginning of the XIX century.

The oldest historic remains of the city correspond to the muslim period. The ''Torre del Oro'' which along with a similar one situated on the opposite bank of the river Guadalquivir, were part of the deffensive system of the port, these two towers were joined by large chains in order to prevent access of any enemy ships.

The Giralda, the old minaret of the no longer standing mosque is 117 mts. high dominating the city and complements the cathedral's beauty. This was built in the XV century on the site of the old mosque; its style is late gothic and its magnitude is only surpassed by Saint Peter's in **Rome** and Saint Paul's in **London**. Its building was began in 1401 and the sculptured alterpiece of its main chapel is the largest of all Spain. There are a great number of religious monuments outstanding more for their paintings and sculptures than their architecture. Among these the church del Sagrario, the temple of El Salvador, the church of Santa Ana, the temple of La Magdalena, the church of San Lorenzo and the convent of Santa Paula.

La Cathedral of Seville

Cathedral. Several interior views

Among the civil buildings, the town hall built under **Carlos V** deserves mention; the Hospital de la Caridad built in 1647 the Hospital de los Venerables also from XV century and the Hospital de la Sangre. During the reign of **Felipe II** the Lonja de Mercaderes was built (1572-1598) where the Indian Archives would be kept, under **Carlos III**. The most important documents of the conquest and colonisation of America are still kept there, complemented with the Biblioteca Colombina (Colombine Library). Another typical example of this period is the ''Fabrica de Tabaco'' (Tobacco Factory), at present occupied by the university. The Casa de Pilatos dated from the XVI century contains many examples of roman archaelogy. The Palacio de las Dueñas from the XV century and the Palacio de San Telmo to which once belonged the Jardines de María Luisa (Gardens). The most representative popular architecture is the jewish quarters (Barrio de Santa Cruz), A laberynth of narrow streets. Among the museums of **Seville,** the Museum of Fine Arts deserves a special mention.

This museum has the second largest collection of paintings in Spain, after the Prado Museum. The Provincial Museum of Archaelogy with examples of roman busts, ceramics, mosaique and medieval archaelogy; the Museum of Contemporary Art which conserves works of art of the XX Century.

Alcalá de Guadaira, Carmona, Cazalla, Dos Hermanas, Ecija, Osuna and **Utrera** are other cities with a historic-touristic interest.

The **Natural Park of Sierra Norte** is situated to the north of **Seville,** and spreads through Park of Sierra Morena. It has an area of 165.000 hectares of smooth downs with beautiful pasture lands covered in evergreen oaks, cork trees and gall-oaks. Among the Park's fauna the black stork and the imperial eagle deserve mention.

Plaza de España square

▼Plaza de España square▲

María Luisa gardens

Itálica. Roman Circus

Itálica. Moisaiques

La Cartuja

Torre del Oro

Los Reales Alcázares

La Cartuja from the Barqueta bridge ▼

La Cartuja. Interior

Juan De Austria fountain ▼

Courtyardin Santa Cruz neighbourhood

María Luisa gardens

Santo Domingo convent. Cloiser

Osuna

Cabildo Eclesiástico. Front

Courtyard in La Encarnación convent ▼

▲ La Colegiata. Interior ▼

▲ Carmona ▼

El Garrobo. Landscape ▼

El Garrobo

Carmona. Door of Seville

Carmona. Panoramic view of the city ▼

Carmona. Tower of Pedro I

Marchena. Arch of the roses

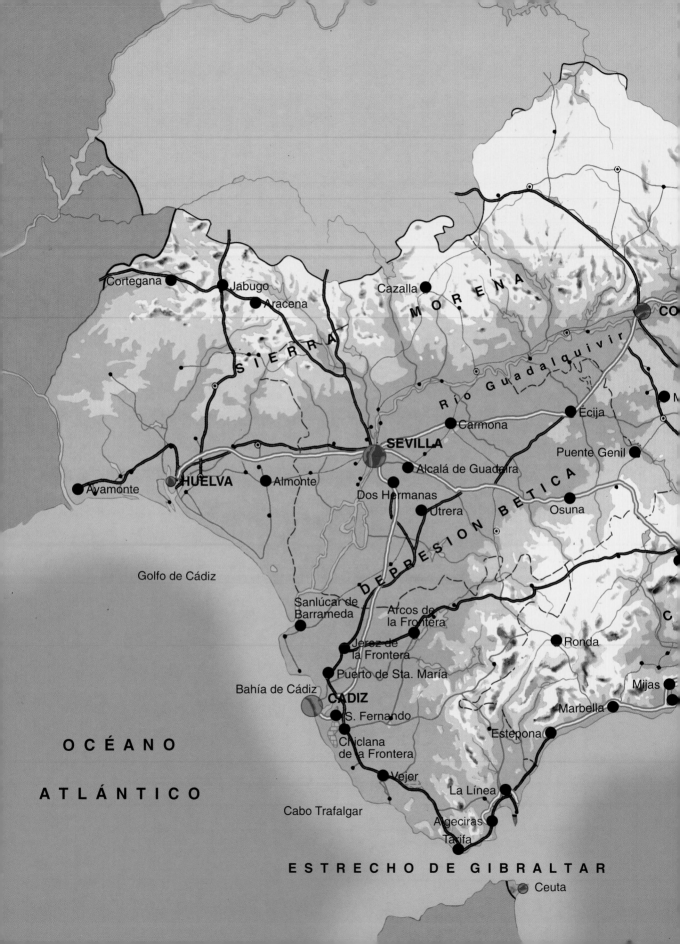

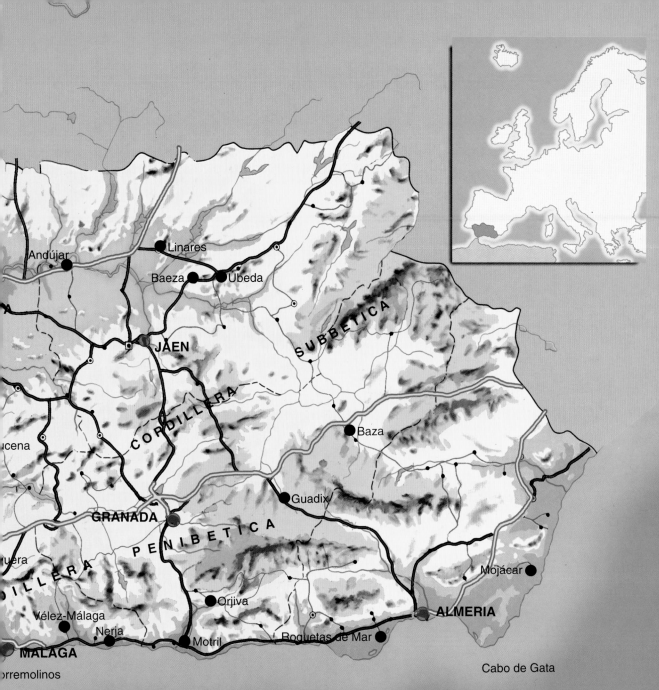

Andújar

Linares

Baeza · Úbeda

JAEN

SUBBÉTICA

CORDILLERA

Baza

ucena

Guadix

GRANADA

PENIBÉTICA

DILLERA

Mojácar

uera

Vélez-Málaga

Orjiva

ALMERIA

Nerja

Motril

Roquetas de Mar

MÁLAGA

Cabo de Gata

rremolinos

rola

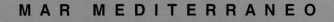

MAR MEDITERRANEO

Cover: Fuente de Piedra lagoon (Málaga). Beach at the Cape of Trafalgar (Cádiz)

Backpage: La Calahorra (Granada)